# Your Amazing Itty Bitty®
# "Before" Financial Checklist:

## *15 Important Actions to Complete Before the Loss of a Loved One*

This book will help you if you:

- are starting to help your aging parents
- are over 50 or retired and beginning to think about the second half of your life
- have been through a rough estate settling process and vowed to never put your family through the same experience
- are any age and trying to get your financial house in order

Using the information in this Itty Bitty® Book, you can get financially organized, update your documents, and have peace of mind that your wishes will be carried out as cost-effectively as possible.

**If you want to save time, stress, money and preserve family relationships in the end, pick up a copy of this helpful Itty Bitty® Book today.**

# Your Amazing Itty Bitty® "Before" Financial Checklist:

*15 Important Actions to Complete Before the Loss of a Loved One*

Marie Burns, CFP®

Published by Itty Bitty® Publishing
A subsidiary of S & P Productions, Inc.

Copyright © 2018 **Marie Burns**

Printed in the United States of America

Itty Bitty® Publishing
311 Main Street, Suite D
El Segundo, CA 90245
(310) 640-8885


ISBN: 978-0-9996519 -2-6

This booklet is intended to be informational only and is not intended to be construed as tax, financial or legal advice. Readers should consult their own advisors who are licensed in their state and are familiar with their personal situation.

*Dedication*

*This book is dedicated to the families I have helped over the years who in the process inspired me to write this book.*

Stop by our Itty Bitty® website to find interesting information regarding the "Before" Financial Checklist:

www.IttyBittyPublishing.com

Or visit **Marie Burns** at

www.**MindMoneyMotion**.com

# Table of Contents

# Introduction

This Itty Bitty Book will guide you in completing 15 important actions that will help you update your financial records before you're gone, which will save:

- stress
- time
- money

and help preserve family relationships.

Remember the old joke: How do you eat an elephant? Answer: One bite at a time. This book breaks down the updating of your financial records into small "bites," so it doesn't feel so overwhelming and you are more likely to take action on implementing the necessary steps.

Being humans, we tend to procrastinate, especially when everything is going well. But during the calm (before the storm) is the best time to think clearly and act rationally to put your financial house in order.

**Those who fail to plan, should plan to fail.**

# Step 1
## Organize:
## Get Your Ducks in a Row

The more you organize your records in advance, the easier it will be for others to deal with after you're gone. Categorize as much as you can in one location (use hanging files, binders, electronic files, whatever you prefer).

1.  Designate major filing sections: banking, debt, employee benefits, estate planning, health, household, insurance, investments, miscellaneous, personal property, real estate, retirement income, school, taxes.
2.  Within each major section, you may want a separate file for sub-categories. Also, pictures or a video of household items are helpful in the personal property section.
3.  Once the files are created, sort and file or scan all documents or statements into the appropriate file.
4.  After filing is complete, keep up with filing additional documents as you receive them.

# Filing Section Sub-Category Examples:

- Debt: car loan, credit card, mortgage, student loan
- Health: dental, medical, vision
- Household: appliances, computer, furniture, phone
- Insurance: auto, home, life, long-term care, umbrella
- Investments: annuity, employer plan, IRA/Roth account, non-retirement account
- Personal property: boat, guns, jewelry, vehicle
- Real estate: primary home, second home, rental, land
- Retirement income: Military, Pension, Social Security (if you haven't already, go to ssa.gov to set up your username and password so you can download a current Social Security statement annually)

# Step 2
## Organize:
## I Own, I Owe

Compile a list of everything you own and update it at least annually. Your goal is to summarize in one place the value of everything you own, as well as everything you owe (known as a Net Worth Statement).

1. Check online for examples of a Net Worth Statement format.
2. Date the Net Worth Statement and list all items or account names (referred to as assets) and their current market values, as well as balances owed (referred to as liabilities).

## Tips for Compiling Your Net Worth Statement

- Make sure the account names listed match the company name shown at the top of the statements they reference. For example, if you have a Roth IRA statement from E-trade, list it on the Net Worth Statement as E-trade Roth IRA, followed by your name.

- Specify account ownership type in the account names whenever possible. For example, if you have a joint investment account at Fidelity, list it as a Joint Fidelity account on the Net Worth Statement.

- If applicable, you may want to itemize the contents of your safe deposit box at the bank and file that list in your banking file. Unless there are valuable items like jewelry, coins, etc., the safe deposit box items (often mainly documents) won't be listed on the Net Worth Statement.

# Step 3
## Organize:
## The Magic Words

As kids, remember the magic word was always "please." These days the magic words are: your username and password. Having a password inventory has become a critical part of accessing family financial records, so you need to have a list of all your login information compiled for when you are no longer around:

1. Save your password list in one preferred place (document on your computer, app on your phone, password inventory booklet).
2. Keep passwords confidential and do not store them in an easily accessible or obvious location.
3. Update your password inventory each time you are forced to change your login information.

## Password Inventory Tips

- List the website address, username and password for each entry.
- If there is a Notes section in your password inventory, you may want to cross-reference the name of the account(s) you are able to access for each entry.
- Include answers to security questions for each site, if applicable.
- Be sure appropriate family members know where to find this inventory when needed.

# Step 4
## Organize:
## Who, What, When, Where, Why

Don't leave family members in the lurch when it comes to paying bills or notifying your creditors. Take the detective work out of it for them by maintaining a list of all common household expenses. Best to include the following details:

1. Who---name of company that gets paid
2. What---dollar amount to be paid
3. When---date expense is to be paid
4. Where---specify whether a check is mailed, the biller auto-deducts, or the payer manually pays online, etc.
5. Why---the service or product being provided

## Wow, You Are Amazing!

By this point, you have already…

- Caught up on all your filing and organized your records into one location.
- Summarized in one list the assets you own and liabilities you owe (Net Worth Statement).
- Compiled a "cheat sheet" of the required login information for all of your accounts (Password Inventory).
- Collected all the necessary details in one spreadsheet or list of the common household bills.

You are on a roll and to be commended! Don't stop now…the organizing is almost done! One more step.

# Step 5
## Organize:
## Inventory the "What Ifs"

The concept of having any insurance policy in place is to transfer the financial risk to an insurance company in case one of the dreaded "what ifs" in life occur (What if I die prematurely? What if I become disabled? What if I need long-term care?). Make a list of the insurance policies covering your risks.

1. Consider a bullet point list of policies that includes the company name, policy number, coverage amount and company/agent phone number.
2. Or you could use a spreadsheet format. Either way, specify the type of insurance.
3. An insurance folder containing just the declaration page from each policy (which captures most of the necessary detail) is another option to consolidate your insurance coverage in one place.

## Your Insurance Policies

Common insurance policy categories:

- Accident
- Auto
- Disability (short- and long-term)
- Health/dental/vision
- Home
- Life
- Long-term care
- Umbrella liability

Don't forget the small policies like the $1,000 death benefit on some bank accounts or credit cards.

Organizing is done! Now on to the homework.

# Step 6
## Homework:
## What's in a Name?

How you name/hold title to your assets, can significantly impact how they are treated after your death. Spending some time with your legal advisor to review the title of each asset on your Net Worth Statement, is an important discussion.

1. You need to decide where you want each asset or account to go after you are gone.
2. Then your legal advisor can help you advise the best way to title each asset so it gets there with the least cost and/or delay.
3. In general, a beneficiary designation on an account bypasses probate and allows that account or policy balance to go directly to the beneficiary.
4. An attorney licensed in your state of residence and who specializes in estate planning is the best resource for getting this advice because each state can have different laws.

## Ways to Title Assets and Bypass the Additional Cost/Delay of Probate—THIS IS WHERE MOST PEOPLE FAIL!

- Joint with rights of survivorship ownership on non-retirement assets
- Payable on Death (POD) designation on bank accounts: savings, money market, CDs
- Transfer on Death (TOD) designation on non-retirement accounts: individual or jointly held stock, mutual fund, and/or bond accounts
- Transfer on Death (TOD) designation on a home, vehicle or property, also called a beneficiary deed
- Title the asset in the name of a trust
- Name primary and contingent beneficiaries on retirement accounts, annuities and life insurance policies (naming your estate as a beneficiary will NOT bypass probate)

Remember, a beneficiary designation is like a mini-will on each account. Each account will get distributed to the beneficiary on that account and it will never go to your will for distribution (unless your estate is listed as beneficiary but then it goes through probate first!), so keep beneficiary designations current and use Trust, TOD or POD in the account titling as recommended by your estate planning attorney.

# Step 7
## Homework:
## The Legal Documents

The main reason to meet with a legal advisor is to draft or update your estate planning documents. The basic legal documents give instructions about what you want to happen with your assets after you are gone. They typically include a will and/or trust, Durable (Financial) Power of Attorney, and Health Care Power of Attorney.

1. Do you need a will or a trust? Estate Tax laws have changed over the years. Your wishes and desire/need for control must be factored into your legal advisor's recommendation on this question.
2. The Power of Attorney documents clarify who you want to make financial or health care decisions for you when you are alive but unable to act (if you are in a coma, for example).
3. Your agent for health care does not need to be the same person as your agent for financial power. Sometimes the one who you want to pay bills is not the same person you want to pull the plug!

## Estate Planning Document Reminders

- When choosing your executor/personal representative/successor trustee, choose someone who is not only honest, but also organized with communication skills; a non-family member (fiduciary or corporate trustee) may make sense instead or jointly with a family member.
- Discuss whether your Durable (Financial) Power of Attorney should be immediate or "springing" (springs into action only at the time of incapacity). As we get older and/or for couples, immediate may be the best option but discuss with your attorney for the best advice regarding your situation.
- Review estate planning documents every 3-5 years, whenever there has been a law change, or when you have had a change in your circumstances.
- The best resource for this legal advice is an attorney who specializes in estate planning and is licensed in your state.
- Attorneys will remind you that you can write, date and sign a Disposition of Personal Property at any time to attach to your estate planning documents. This separate list itemizes things you specifically want to go to certain people (i.e. china to daughter, gun to son, piano to school, etc.)

# Step 8
## Homework:
## The Morbid Details

Have you thought through or talked with family about your wishes related to organ donation? Burial vs. cremation? Service preferences? Writing down your desires related to final details saves family from guessing what you wanted.

1.  Most states have a Final Disposition form or something similar so you can clarify your thoughts on burial vs. cremation, ceremony preference, organ donation, burial/ashes location, etc. in writing.
2.  You may want to purchase a burial plot, tombstone, or mausoleum in advance to eliminate one more detail for family.
3.  Some states or attorneys make a wallet card available to carry with you that identifies your health care agent.
4.  Is there a desire to write an ethical will? An ethical will is like a legacy letter, a way to pass on your values, lessons you learned from life, or forgiveness of family or friends.

## Final Celebration

Sometimes when an illness is involved, the terminal loved one may want to be involved in the final celebration planning, which could include:

- Selecting the location
- Planning the music
- Creating a menu
- Writing an obituary
- Leaving letters or making phone calls to loved ones
- Sharing memories, scriptures, photos, poems, quotes, advice
- Check out www.funerals.org for other planning considerations

# Step 9
## Homework:
## To Each His Own

There may come a time when you need your Durable (Financial) Power of Attorney to act on your behalf while you are alive. Each financial institution will have its own paperwork requirement, so it's good to become familiar with what that entails in advance.

1.  To be aware of the process and time frame that may be involved with needing your financial agent to act on your behalf, you may want to begin asking your bank, investment and retirement account providers what they require to name a financial power of attorney with them.
2.  Each institution is likely to require their own form and will not just accept a copy of your Durable (Financial) Power of Attorney document.
3.  Consider when you may want to initiate the financial power of attorney authorization process with each institution to avoid a delay at a more crucial time.

**Incapacity**

Before anything happens and a Durable (Financial) Power of Attorney authorization is needed, it is a good idea to make sure the person you named to make your decisions:

- is aware of your wishes and has a copy of the Durable Power of Attorney document
- knows where the original document is located
- has signature authority on a bank account
- if applicable, knows the location of, and has the ability to access, your safe deposit box and where the key is located

Consider travelling with a "To Go" bag that contains important information like a copy of your Power of Attorney documents, medication list, and ICE (In Case of Emergency) contact sheet.

# Step 10
## Homework: Who Gets What?

Remember that each beneficiary designation dictates the distribution of each account so make sure all of your beneficiary designations are current. Too often we list someone – then, life changes, people pass away, or relationships change, so your beneficiary designations may need to change too.

1. Consider naming primary and contingent beneficiaries on all accounts and policies. A contingent beneficiary specifies who would receive the account if both you and the primary beneficiary perished in a car accident together, for example.
2. We are usually aware of the need to designate beneficiaries on retirement accounts, life insurance policies and annuities but you should also confirm they are current.
3. You can name beneficiaries on non-retirement accounts, i.e. POD (Payable on Death) on bank accounts and TOD (Transfer on Death) on investment accounts and property.
4. Pets are not usually beneficiaries, but be sure you specify their needs and your wishes with family and in your will/trust.

## Beneficiary Designations

- The best person to give you advice on naming beneficiaries is your legal advisor. He/she understands the big picture of your estate and knows what it is you are trying to accomplish.
- Discuss with your attorney the option to add "per stirpes" or "by rights of representation" wording (the ability to include grandchildren if their parents predecease you) to a beneficiary designation.

Too often, people misunderstand and believe that once their will or trust is drafted, that takes care of everything and that beneficiary designations don't matter because they have it all spelled out in their will or trust. But remember, a beneficiary designation acts like a little mini-will in dictating where each account gets distributed, so the account never references the will or trust for distribution instructions at all on most accounts unless the will or trust is listed as the beneficiary (and that may not be the best practice for tax reasons) or goes through probate because there was no beneficiary listed.

You need to consult your legal advisor for beneficiary designation recommendations – don't guess!

# Step 11
## Homework:
## Monthly Moolah

When life suddenly changes, survivors or family members may need access to cash temporarily or need increased income for a short or long period of time. It's good to be aware of, or to consider putting some options in place in advance to address these potential income needs.

1.  In the case of a couple, household Social Security income goes down after one passes away. The surviving spouse gets to continue receiving the higher of the two Social Security payments and the other payment stops.
2.  Pension income often stops or is reduced after the death of the original recipient.
3.  If you own a home, it may be wise to talk with your bank about setting up a HELOC (Home Equity Line of Credit) if not already in place, for immediate access to cash if/when needed.
4.  Sometimes a reverse mortgage can be explored to leverage the value of a home as an ongoing income source (consult a tax advisor if looking into this option).

## Social Security

As this program's rules evolve, these rules of thumb can change:

- For couples, it is often best for the higher income earner, if healthy, to delay taking the retirement benefit until as close to age 70 as possible to maximize the benefit for the surviving spouse down the road.
- If you live to your mid 80s or beyond, you will receive more lifetime income from Social Security if you delay taking your benefit until closer to or at age 70.
- Your Social Security benefit increases in value by 8% per year that you delay it, up to the age of 70 (so there is no benefit to waiting beyond age 70).
- Social Security was designed to provide about 1/3 of what a retiree may need to live on.
- Several factors should be considered with your financial advisor in determining the best claiming age: health, family longevity, other income sources, tax bracket now and later, Required Minimum Distributions, employment plans, survivor's situation and Roth conversion opportunities.

# Step 12
## Homework:
## K.I.S.S.

The acronym K.I.S.S. stands for Keep It Super Simple (or Keep It Simple, Stupid!). Whatever you can do to simplify your financial situation in advance, will not only benefit you, but will mean less time and paperwork for your family later as well.

1. Consolidate your accounts. If you have more than one of the same type of account, ask yourself if that is necessary. It may make sense to combine similar types of accounts into one.
2. If you hold paper stock certificates, think about combining them in book entry form instead into a single account as this would mean less work for heirs down the road.
3. Close or consolidate small accounts.

## Whew, The Homework is Done!

You should feel very proud of yourself for every step you have taken to get this far. Anything you have completed puts you in a better position than before you started and your family will thank you too.

- Life is full of surprises – not all of them are welcome.
- Working with licensed tax, legal and financial advisors is the smaller price to pay along the way than the costly mistakes, taxes, losses you or your family may experience without that advice.
- If incapacity or the end is near, there are a few more actions to consider…

# Step 13
## The End is Near:
## The Tax Expert

No one wants to pay more taxes than required, at any time of life. There may be a few tax-saving opportunities that can be lost at death if not acted upon before death, so you should meet with your tax advisor to discuss as the laws do change.

1. Meet with your tax advisor to update him/her on the potential terminal or incapacity situation.
2. Inquire about whether there are any unrealized gains that should be realized in order to use up any tax loss carryovers from previous years that could otherwise be lost upon death.
3. Same question with charitable contribution carryovers that could be lost upon death.
4. Consult your tax advisor for any additional tax planning considerations allowable by current law.

## Choosing a Tax Advisor

- Just like looking for a mechanic, hairdresser, dentist, etc., DO ask people you know who they work with and would recommend.
- Because you want to meet in person, DON'T call to set an introductory (complementary) appointment during the busiest times of the year (April 15, October 15 and year-end).
- Since you are looking for someone who works with people in your situation, DO ask for a description of their typical client.
- DON'T forget to provide copies of your last two years of tax returns in advance of the meeting in order to ask for a tax preparation fee estimate.

# Step 14
## The End is Near:
## The Legal Expert

So many clichés in life end up being so true, including the one that reminds us "we get what we pay for." Don't try to take any shortcuts with your estate planning – see an attorney.

1. Ongoing visits with an estate planning attorney, especially near the end, will be invaluable in getting things where you want them to go with the least cost and delay.
2. Estate planning documents are less likely to be contested if drafted by an attorney vs. a fill-in-the-blank will/trust kit.
3. Gifting limits and charitable contributions can be thought through more thoroughly.
4. Direct payments to medical, dental or educational institutions (none of which count toward the annual gift exclusion amount) may make sense to consider.

## Choosing an Estate Planning Attorney

- To find an estate planning attorney, get referrals from people you know.
- Meet with two or three attorneys (a complementary introductory meeting) who specialize in estate planning to understand the fees and get a gut check on how you might feel working with any of them.
- Ask for their thoughts about who needs a trust vs. a will and understand how they charge (flat fee or hourly).

# Step 15
## The End is Near:
## The Planning Expert

The tax advisor helps consider taxes, the legal expert gives advice based on the law, but there is no one overseeing the big picture of your financial life with you so consider working with a financial advisor.

1. A CFP, Certified Financial Planner, has a fiduciary duty to advise on what is in your best interest.
2. For help acting on the tax and legal advisor's advice, as well as to consider all areas of financial planning, a CFP® can be your advocate and assist in communicating and implementing the advice of the team of advisors.
3. It's tough; we sometimes don't want our children too involved, this is not an area we are comfortable talking about in detail with other family or friends, so who else can we turn to?
4. You need someone licensed (so you are protected), experienced (so you are not the guinea pig) and trustworthy (so you don't get hurt), who will care about, and help to take care of your financial needs.

## What a CFP® Can Help With

- Estate Planning---assisting with updating beneficiaries, account titling, and charitable/gifting based on the advice of your estate planning attorney and tax advisor.

- Education Planning---understanding and investing in college funding options.

- Income Planning---income and expense planning with prudent withdrawal strategies in conjunction with a tax advisor.

- Investment Planning---monitoring and advising on investing for growth and income in coordination with your tax advisor.

- Insurance Planning---analyzing options to address risks associated with death, long term care and disability.

- Retirement Planning---lifestyle planning to meet spending goals and needs in retirement to minimize the worry about running out of money.

**You've finished. Before you go...**

Tweet/share that you finished this book.

Please star rate this book.

Reviews are solid gold to writers. Please take a few minutes to give us some itty bitty feedback.

## ABOUT THE AUTHOR

Marie Burns started her career helping people balance their diet and exercise as a Registered Dietitian. A dozen years later, she began her journey as a Certified Financial Planner™ Professional and has been helping people balance their finances for almost two decades. Both roles involve guiding others to make behavior changes.

As the oldest of four children as well as the mother of four children, she is a natural fit for serving others as their "financial mother." Coming into the financial industry as a second career has helped Marie avoid the lingo of finance-speak and instead focus on translating complex subjects into understandable English.

When Marie realized that she was getting questions DAILY from friends, clients, and family related to helping aging parents, settling family estates, and couples worrying about how things will go when one of them is no longer around, she knew she needed to write a financial checklist.

Marie's goal is to create The Ripple Effect: these financial checklist books act like a rock launched into a pond and its ripples reach many more lives than she could ever positively impact in person. Marie writes and speaks to groups at www.MindMoneyMotion.com. She advises clients at www.FocusPointPlanning.com.

If you liked this Itty Bitty® Book, you might also enjoy…

- **Your Amazing Itty Bitty® "After" Financial Checklist: 15 Important Actions to Complete After the Loss of a Loved One–** Marie Burns

- **Your Amazing Itty Bitty® Book of Getting Financially Organized–** Marie Burns

- **Your Amazing Itty Bitty® "Before" and "After" Death Financial Checklists (three books in one) –** Marie Burns

And many other Itty Bitty® Books available online